Cursive Writing II

II

Reference Workbook

Doreen S. Castillio

authorHOUSE®

AuthorHouse™
1663 Liberty Drive
Bloomington, IN 47403
www.authorhouse.com
Phone: 833-262-8899

Published by AuthorHouse 05/19/2022

ISBN: 978-1-6655-5943-0 (sc)
ISBN: 978-1-6655-5944-7 (e)

Library of Congress Control Number: 2022909149

CONTENTS

SECTION ONE

INTRODUCTION

a c u i m n o r s u v w x ß | 13

b d h k l t | 6

PREVIEW

g j p q y z | 6

f | 1

A B C D E F G H I K L M N
O P Q R S T U V W X | 23
Y Y Z | 3

aceimnorsuvwxz 14

bdfhklt 7

gjpqy 5

ABCDEFGHIJKLMNO

PQRSTUVWXYZ 26

RULE Move from dot to arrow.

RULE *Do not erase. Keep on writing.
Use a pen or eraserless pencil.

Print/
Manuscript   Cursive

Top Line

Space One

RULE Retracing - means to stop and go back.
→over a line.

*retracing
will be a bold line.

not
retracing

Use 4 lines and 3 spaces
Look here
to place letters.

Middle Line

Space Two

RULE

Bottom Line

10 RULES

Space Three

Below The Bottom Line

RULE Go from
Practice Line - Big

RULE Letter endings
have   tails   or   smiley faces

—which act as spaces between letters.

RULE Common
Errors,
DO NOT
COPY.

RULE Some CAPITALS → may not join letters.

to↓

Practice Lines - Small.

RULE The boat comes last.   boat boat

RULE Slant depends on → right or left,
handedness.

top line

middle line

bottom line

below the bottom line

slant

cursive starts with c

space 1

space 2

space 3

tail

smiley face

short letters

tall letters

below the bottom line letters

SECTION TWO

LEARNING LOWERCASE LETTERS
FROM SIMPLE TO DIFFICULT SHAPES
Order of Letters

Move from dot to arrow.

Print/
Manuscript

Cursive

*Do <u>not</u> erase. Keep on writing.
Use a pen or eraserless pencil.

Top Line

Space One

<u>Middle</u> <u>Line</u>

Space Two

Bottom Line

Space Three

Below The Bottom Line

<u>Practice</u> <u>Line</u> - <u>Big</u>

Common
Errors

DO <u>NOT</u>
COPY

started in
wrong place

too
close

top
wide

<u>Practice</u> <u>Lines</u> - <u>Small</u>

Move from dot to arrow.

*Do not erase. Keep on writing.
Use a pen or eraserless pencil.

Print/
Manuscript   Cursive   Top Line

                                                                     Space One

                                                                     Middle Line

                                                                     Space Two

                                                                     Bottom Line

                                                                     Space Three

                                                                     Below The Bottom Line

Practice Line - Big

Common
Errors   pointy   do not retrace   top wide
DO NOT
COPY

need to
retrace

Practice Lines - Small

Move from dot to arrow.

Print/
Manuscript

Cursive

*Do not erase. Keep on writing.
Use a pen or eraserless pencil.

Top Line

Space One

smiley

loop is okay

Middle Line

Space Two

Bottom Line

Space Three

Below The Bottom Line

Practice Line — Big

Common Errors
DO NOT COPY

pointy

too wide
too short

not round

too wide

Practice Lines — Small

Move from dot to arrow.

*Do not erase. Keep on writing.
Use a pen or eraserless pencil.

Print/ Manuscript	Cursive		Top Line
			Space One
			Middle Line
			Space Two
			Bottom Line
			Space Three
			Below The Bottom Line

Practice Line - Big

Common Errors
DO NOT COPY

too wide

slants left

no space

cross too high

start in the wrong place

Practice Lines - Small

Move from dot to arrow.

*Do not erase. Keep on writing.
Use a pen or eraserless pencil.

Print/Manuscript   Cursive   Top Line

Space One

Middle Line

Space Two

Bottom Line

Space Three

Below The Bottom Line

Practice Line - Big

Common Errors   pointy
DO NOT COPY   too wide   needs to be wider
wrong slant   cross too high   need space

Practice Lines - Small

Move from dot to arrow.

*Do not erase. Keep on writing.
Use a pen or eraserless pencil.

Print/
Manuscript

Cursive

Top Line

Space One

Middle Line

Space Two

Bottom Line

Space Three

Below The Bottom Line

Practice Line - Big

Common
Errors

touch
top

pointy

too
wide

too
narrow

DO NOT
COPY

pointy

Practice Lines - Small

Move from dot to arrow.

*Do not erase. Keep on writing. Use a pen or eraserless pencil.

Print/ Manuscript

Cursive

Top Line

Space One

Middle Line

Space Two

Bottom Line

Space Three

Below The Bottom Line

Practice Line - Big

Common Errors
DO NOT COPY

too short   too long

top long   do not meet ends

wrong starting point

too wide retrace more down

Practice Lines - Small

caoeldt

caoeldt

caoeldt

cat

toad

cocoa

all

dot

tate

tate

total

doodle

Move from dot to arrow.

Print/
Manuscript   Cursive

*Do not erase. Keep on writing.
Use a pen or eraserless pencil.

Top Line

Space One

Middle Line

Space Two

Bottom Line

Space Three

Below The Bottom Line

Practice Line - Big

Common
Errors
DO NOT
COPY

retrace too much space

point make a bump

slant this line

Practice Lines - Small

Move from dot to arrow.   *Do not erase. Keep on writing.
Print/   Use a pen or eraserless pencil.
Manuscript   Cursive   Top Line
_____

                                                          Space One
-    Middle Line

                                                          Space Two

                                                          Bottom Line

                                                          Space Three

                                                          Below The Bottom Line
_____

Practice Line - Big
_____
- -

_____

Common   retrace   too much   too
Errors   ↓   space   wide
DO NOT
COPY
                        touch   no slant
                        line
_____

Practice Lines - Small
- -

_____
- -

_____

caoldtnm

mo on

can ten

me mad

motename

dont motel

Move from dot to arrow.   *Do not erase. Keep on writing.
                                            Use a pen or eraserless pencil.

Print/
Manuscript   Cursive   Top Line

                                                                Space One

                                                                Middle Line

                                                                Space Two

                                                                Bottom Line

                                                                Space Three

                                                                Below The Bottom Line

Practice Line - Big

Common
Errors   too wide   retrace
                 too long   no space
DO NOT
COPY

                        wrong start

Practice Lines - Small

Move from dot to arrow.

*Do not erase. Keep on writing.
Use a pen or eraserless pencil.

Print/ Manuscript	Cursive		Top Line
			Space One
			Middle Line
			Space Two
			Bottom Line
			Space Three
			Below The Bottom Line

Practice Line - Big

Common Errors DO NOT COPY

too small

too big

scoop

no tracing

Practice Lines - Small

caoeldtnmhk

hat thank

catchdock

hotmock

health

tackle

Move from dot to arrow.

*Do not erase. Keep on writing.
Use a pen or eraserless pencil.

Print/
Manuscript

Cursive

Top Line

Space One

When u starts a word,
add an extra stroke.

Middle Line

Space Two

Bottom Line

Space Three

Below The Bottom Line

Practice Line - Big

Common
Errors

too narrow   too wide

DO NOT
COPY

retrace

Practice Lines - Small

Move from dot to arrow.

Print/
Manuscript

Cursive

*Do not erase. Keep on writing.
Use a pen or eraserless pencil.

When w starts a word,
add an extra stroke.

Top Line

Space One

Middle Line

Space Two

Bottom Line

Space Three

Below The Bottom Line

Practice Line - Big

Common
Errors

DO NOT
COPY

too wide

too narrow

too long

too short

too much space
retrace

Practice Lines - Small

Move from dot to arrow.

*Do not erase. Keep on writing.
Use a pen or eraserless pencil.

Print/
Manuscript

Cursive

Top Line

Space One

Middle Line

Space Two

Bottom Line

Space Three

Below The Bottom Line

Practice Line - Big

Common
Errors
DO NOT
COPY

• too high
too wide

• too low
too narrow

wrong
starting
point

retrace

Practice Lines - Small

Move from dot to arrow.

*Do not erase. Keep on writing.
Use a pen or eraserless pencil.

Print/Manuscript	Cursive		Top Line
			Space One
			Middle Line
			Space Two
			Bottom Line
			Space Three
			Below The Bottom Line

Practice Line - Big

Common
Errors
DO NOT
COPY

too wide

cross at bottom line

narrow bottom

•too high

pointy

too low

•too narrow

Practice Lines - Small

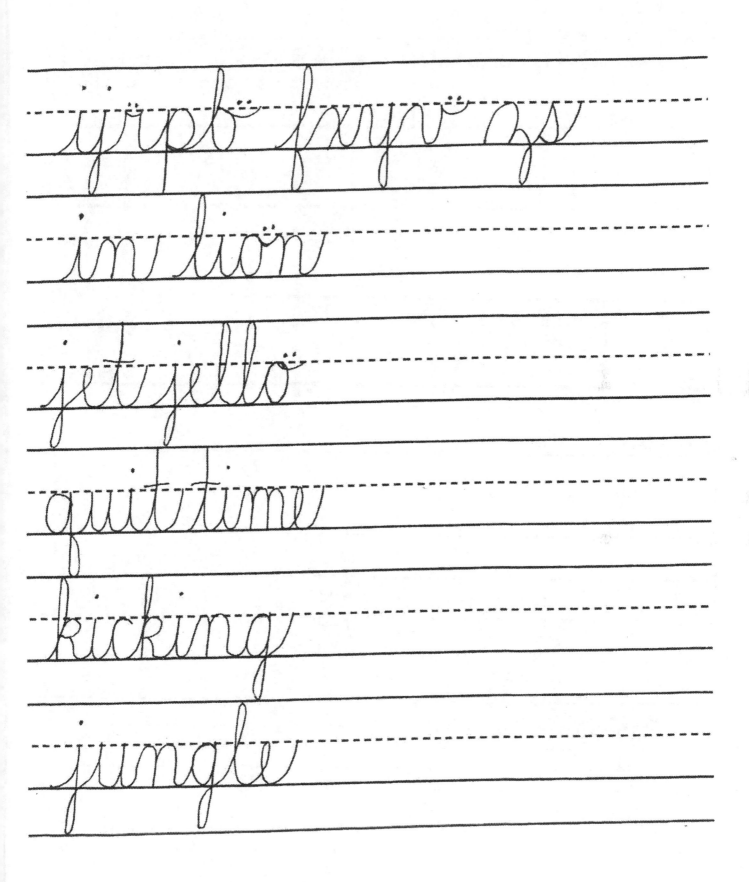

ijrpb fxyv zs

im lion

jet jello

quit time

kicking

jungle

Move from dot to arrow.

*Do not erase. Keep on writing.
Use a pen or eraserless pencil.

Print/Manuscript	Cursive	Top Line
		Space One
		Middle Line
		Space Two
		Bottom Line
		Space Three
		Below The Bottom Line

Practice Line - Big

Common Errors
DO NOT COPY

too wide   too narrow   too wide

too low   wrong direction

Practice Lines - Small

rpb fxyv zs

car near

rice tar

heart

learn

mirror

Move from dot to arrow.   *Do <u>not</u> erase. Keep on writing.
                            Use a pen or eraserless pencil.

Print/
Manuscript   Cursive   Top Line

                                                               Space One

                                                               <u>Middle</u> Line

                                                               Space Two

                                                               Bottom Line

                                                               Space Three

                                                               Below The Bottom Line

Practice Line - Big

Common
Errors   too boxy   should
DO <u>NOT</u>   be round   use
COPY   space three   too small   too big
                                           two and down a
                                           space
                                                                       stay in
                                                                       correct space

Practice Lines - Small

Move from dot to arrow.   *Do not erase. Keep on writing.
                                Use a pen or eraserless pencil.
Print/
Manuscript   Cursive

Top Line

Space One

Middle Line

Space Two

Bottom Line

Space Three

Below The Bottom Line

Practice Line - Big

Common
Errors   too wide
DO NOT   no retracing   open,
COPY   please close

                                      cross
                                      lower

Practice Lines - Small

pb fmyvns

pig pink

apple

peach

pineapple

rabbit

big

boat

bread

habit

right

bought

Move from dot to arrow.

Print/
Manuscript   Cursive

*Do <u>not</u> erase. Keep on writing.
Use a pen or eraserless pencil.

Top Line

Space One

Middle Line

Space Two

Bottom Line

Space Three

Below The Bottom Line

Practice Line - Big

Common
Errors
DO <u>NOT</u>
COPY

too narrow

too wide

← need three
spaces

on the wrong
side

too wide

Practice Lines - Small

Move from dot to arrow.

*Do not erase. Keep on writing. Use a pen or eraserless pencil.

Print/
Manuscript

Cursive

Top Line

Space One

Middle Line

Space Two

Bottom Line

Space Three

Below The Bottom Line

Practice Line - Big

Common Errors DO NOT COPY

cross at wrong line

almost touching other lines

Practice Lines - Small

fxyv zs

forfour

halffawn

oxxviox

twix

axlewax

Move from dot to arrow.

*Do not erase. Keep on writing.
Use a pen or eraserless pencil.

Print/
Manuscript   Cursive   Top Line

                                                               Space One

                                                               Middle Line

                                                               Space Two

                                                               Bottom Line

                                                               Space Three

                                                               Below The Bottom Line

Practice Line - Big

Common
Errors   cross at bottom line   too narrow
DO NOT
COPY   should swing upwards

                ← too wide

Practice Lines - Small

Move from dot to arrow.

Print/
Manuscript   Cursive

*Do <u>not</u> erase. Keep on writing.
Use a pen or eraserless pencil.

<u>Top Line</u>

Space One

<u>Middle Line</u>

Space Two

<u>Bottom Line</u>

Space Three

<u>Below The Bottom Line</u>

<u>Practice Line - Big</u>

Common
Errors
DO <u>NOT</u>
COPY

should be
a point

not pointy   too wide

<u>Practice Lines - Small</u>

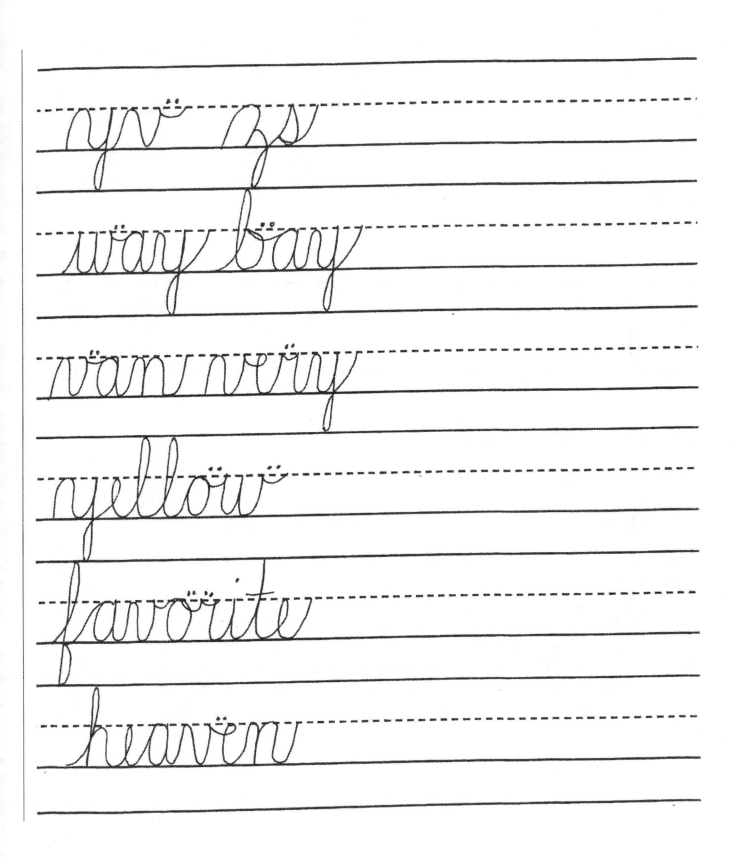

Move from dot to arrow.

Print/
Manuscript Cursive

*Do not erase. Keep on writing.
Use a pen or eraserless pencil.

Top Line

Space One

Middle Line

Space Two

Bottom Line

Space Three

Below The Bottom Line

Practice Line - Big

Common
Errors
DO NOT
COPY

too narrow

cross at line
bottom

should be
narrow

cross at bottom
line

Practice Lines - Small

Move from dot to arrow.

*Do not erase. Keep on writing.
Use a pen or eraserless pencil.

Print/
Manuscript   Cursive   Top Line

fits in a triangle shape   Space One

Middle Line

Space Two

Bottom Line

SpaceThree

Below The Bottom Line

Practice Line - Big

Common
Errors   think   needs a   too narrow
DO NOT   triangle   point   too straight
COPY   lines too straight
                        no loop   too wide
                        retrace

Practice Lines - Small

as

zoo zero

so does

zip zebra

sorry

lizard

SECTION THREE

IN ALPHABETICAL ORDER

Move from dot to arrow.

Print/ Manuscript

Cursive

*Do not erase. Keep on writing. Use a pen or eraserless pencil.

Top Line

Space One

Middle Line

Space Two

Bottom Line

Space Three

Below The Bottom Line

Practice Line - Big

Common Errors DO NOT COPY

too pointy

don't retrace at top

go straight up to top line

too narrow

too big

too narrow

Practice Lines - Small

Move from dot to arrow.

*Do not erase. Keep on writing. Use a pen or eraserless pencil.

Print/ Manuscript

Cursive

Top Line

Space One

Middle Line

Space Two

Bottom Line

Space Three

Below The Bottom Line

Practice Line - Big

retrace - no loop

Common Errors

DO NOT COPY

where's the bottom

big bottom

small bottom

Practice Lines - Small

Move from dot to arrow. *Do not erase. Keep on writing.
Use a pen or eraserless pencil.

Print/
Manuscript   Cursive

Top Line

Space One

Middle Line

Space Two

Bottom Line

Space Three

Below The Bottom Line

Practice Line - Big

Common
Errors

DO NOT
COPY

start in
wrong place

too
wide

too
narrow
tail

Practice Lines - Small

Move from dot to arrow.

Print/Manuscript

Cursive

*Do not erase. Keep on writing.
Use a pen or eraserless pencil.

Top Line

Space One

Middle Line

Space Two

Bottom Line

Space Three

Below The Bottom Line

Practice Line - Big

Common Errors
DO NOT COPY

need slant to right

pointy

too big loop

too big

too round

pointy

big big

Practice Lines - Small

Move from dot to arrow.

*Do not erase. Keep on writing.
Use a pen or eraserless pencil.

Print/
Manuscript   Cursive

	Top Line
	Space One
	Middle Line
	Space Two
	Bottom Line
	Space Three
	Below The Bottom Line

Practice Line - Big

Common
Errors
DO NOT
COPY

too narrow   too wide   do not retrace
retracing
too long

Practice Lines - Small

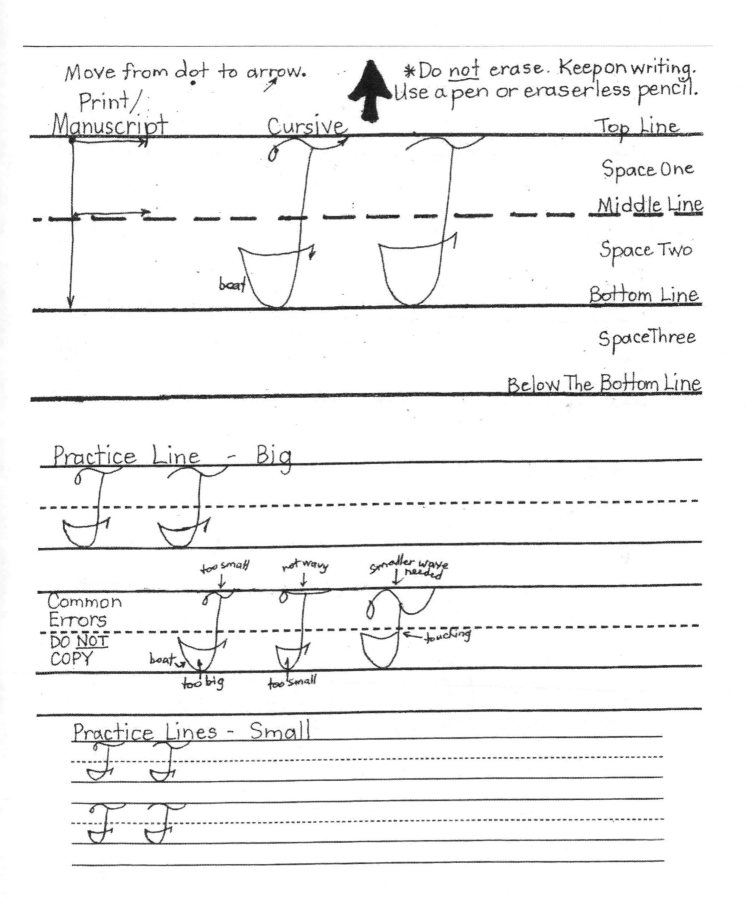

Move from dot to arrow.

*Do not erase. Keep on writing. Use a pen or eraserless pencil.

Print/ Manuscript   Cursive   Top Line

Space One

Middle Line

boat   Space Two

Bottom Line

Space Three

Below The Bottom Line

Practice Line - Big

Common Errors DO NOT COPY

too small   not wavy   smaller wave needed

boat   touching

too big   too small

Practice Lines - Small

Move from dot to arrow.

*Do not erase. Keep on writing.
Use a pen or eraserless pencil.

Print/ Manuscript   Cursive   Top Line

                                                                Space One

                                                                Middle Line

                                                                Space Two

                                                         boat   Bottom Line

                                                                Space Three

                                                                Below The Bottom Line

Practice Line - Big

Common Errors

DO NOT COPY

too narrow   too wide   too close to middle line

not a boat

boat goes out and back in

Practice Lines - Small

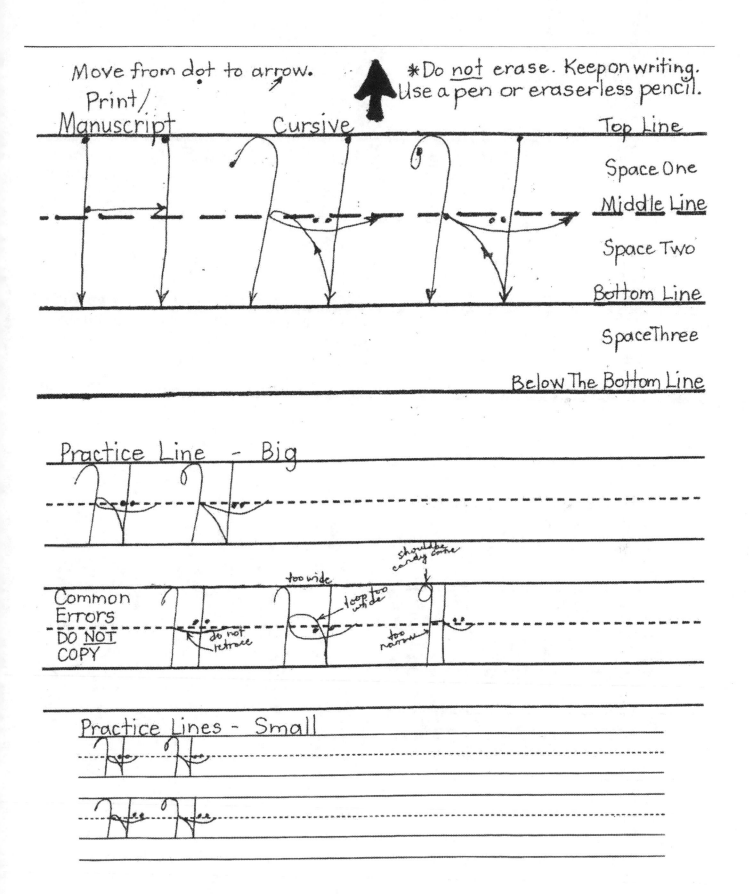

Move from dot to arrow.

*Do not erase. Keep on writing. Use a pen or eraserless pencil.

Print/ Manuscript

Cursive

Top Line

Space One

Middle Line

Space Two

Bottom Line

Space Three

Below The Bottom Line

Practice Line - Big

Common Errors DO NOT COPY

too wide

loop too wide

should be candy cane

do not retrace

too narrow

Practice Lines - Small

Move from dot to arrow.

Print/ Manuscript

Cursive

*Do not erase. Keep on writing. Use a pen or eraserless pencil.

boat→

Top Line

Space One

Middle Line

Space Two

Bottom Line

Space Three

Below The Bottom Line

Practice Line - Big

Common Errors

DO NOT COPY

getthe back stroke

this is the beginning

boat→

curl

Practice Lines - Small

Move from dot to arrow.   *Do not erase. Keep on writing.
                                  Use a pen or eraserless pencil.
Print/   Top Line
Manuscript   Cursive
                                                          Space One
                                                          Middle Line

                                                          Space Two

                                                          Bottom Line

                                                          Space Three

                                                          Below The Bottom Line

Practice Line - Big

Common
Errors   pointy   too   check slant to right
DO NOT   wide
COPY   check   too
            starting point   wide

Practice Lines - Small

Move from dot to arrow.

*Do not erase. Keep on writing.
Use a pen or eraserless pencil.

Print/
Manuscript   Cursive   Top Line

                                                               Space One

                                                               Middle Line

                                                               Space Two

                                                               Bottom Line

                                                               Space Three

                                                               Below The Bottom Line

Practice Line - Big

Common
Errors   not a candy cane   not a candy cane
DO NOT   looks like H   holoop
COPY
                do not retrace   need a bump not a scoop

Practice Lines - Small

Move from dot to arrow.

Print/
Manuscript

Cursive

*Do not erase. Keep on writing.
Use a pen or eraserless pencil.

Top Line

Space One

Middle Line

Space Two

Bottom Line

Space Three

Below The Bottom Line

Practice Line - Big

Common
Errors
DO NOT
COPY

wrong
start

too big

loop goes
wrong
way

should be
lower
not round

stay close
to bottom line

scoop

Practice Lines - Small

Move from dot to arrow.

*Do not erase. Keep on writing.
Use a pen or eraserless pencil.

Print/
Manuscript   Cursive

Top Line

Space One

Middle Line

Space Two

Bottom Line

Space Three

Below The Bottom Line

Practice Line - Big

Common
Errors
DO NOT
COPY

retrace here

too narrow

uneven

start in
middle of
space one

too wide

not a
candy
cane?

Practice Lines - Small

Move from dot to arrow.

*Do not erase. Keep on writing. Use a pen or eraserless pencil.

Print/Manuscript

Cursive

Top Line

Space One

Middle Line

Space Two

Bottom Line

Space Three

Below The Bottom Line

Practice Line - Big

Common Errors
DO NOT COPY

need to retrace

too wide

too narrow

must touch top line

not candy cane

retrace

Practice Lines - Small

Move from dot to arrow.

*Do not erase. Keep on writing.
Use a pen or eraserless pencil.

Print/
Manuscript

Cursive

Top Line

Space One

Middle Line

Space Two

Bottom Line

Space Three

Below The Bottom Line

Practice Line - Big

pointy   too narrow   too short   too long

Common
Errors
DO NOT
COPY

too wide

Practice Lines - Small

Move from dot to arrow.

*Do not erase. Keep on writing.
Use a pen or eraserless pencil.

Print/
Manuscript

Cursive

Top Line

Space One

Middle Line

Space Two

Bottom Line

Space Three

Below The Bottom Line

Practice Line - Big

Common
Errors
DO NOT
COPY

too big

too small

retrace loop
do not loop

Practice Lines - Small

Move from dot to arrow.　　　*Do not erase. Keep on writing.
Use a pen or eraserless pencil.

Print/
Manuscript　　　　Cursive　　　　　　　　　　　Top Line

　　　　　　　　　　　　　　　　　　　　　　　　Space One

　　　　　　　　　　　　　　　　　　　　　　　　Middle Line

　　　　　　　　　　　　　　　　　　　　　　　　Space Two

　　　　　　　　　　　　　　　　　　　　　　　　Bottom Line

　　　　　　　　　　　　　　　　　　　　　　　　Space Three

　　　　　　　　　　　　　　　　　　　　　　　　Below The Bottom Line

Practice Line - Big

Common
Errors
DO NOT
COPY

start on middle line　　　too narrow　　　too wide

loop too high

Practice Lines - Small

Move from dot to arrow.

*Do not erase. Keep on writing. Use a pen or eraserless pencil.

Print/ Manuscript

Cursive

Top Line

Space One

Middle Line

Space Two

Bottom Line

Space Three

Below The Bottom Line

Practice Line - Big

Common Errors

DO NOT COPY

too small

too big

go to middle line

too low

too long

do not retrace

Practice Lines - Small

Move from dot to arrow.

*Do not erase. Keep on writing.
Use a pen or eraserless pencil.

Print/Manuscript   Cursive

Top Line

Space One

Middle Line

Space Two

Bottom Line

Space Three

Below The Bottom Line

boat →

Practice Line - Big

Common Errors

DO NOT COPY

need boat →

top high

top wide

not down — go to the right

Practice Lines - Small

Move from dot to arrow.

Print/
Manuscript

Cursive

*Do not erase. Keep on writing.
Use a pen or eraserless pencil.

Top Line

Space One

Middle Line

Space Two

boat

Bottom Line

Space Three

Below The Bottom Line

Practice Line - Big

Common
Errors

DO NOT
COPY

not loop

not curvy

too short

too high

don't touch

too narrow

Practice Lines - Small

Move from dot to arrow.

*Do not erase. Keep on writing.
Use a pen or eraserless pencil.

Print/
Manuscript   Cursive

Top Line

Space One

Middle Line

Space Two

Bottom Line

Space Three

Below The Bottom Line

Practice Line - Big

not a
configure

too wide

Common
Errors

DO NOT
COPY

too narrow

retrace
here

Practice Lines - Small

Move from dot to arrow.

*Do not erase. Keep on writing.
Use a pen or eraserless pencil.

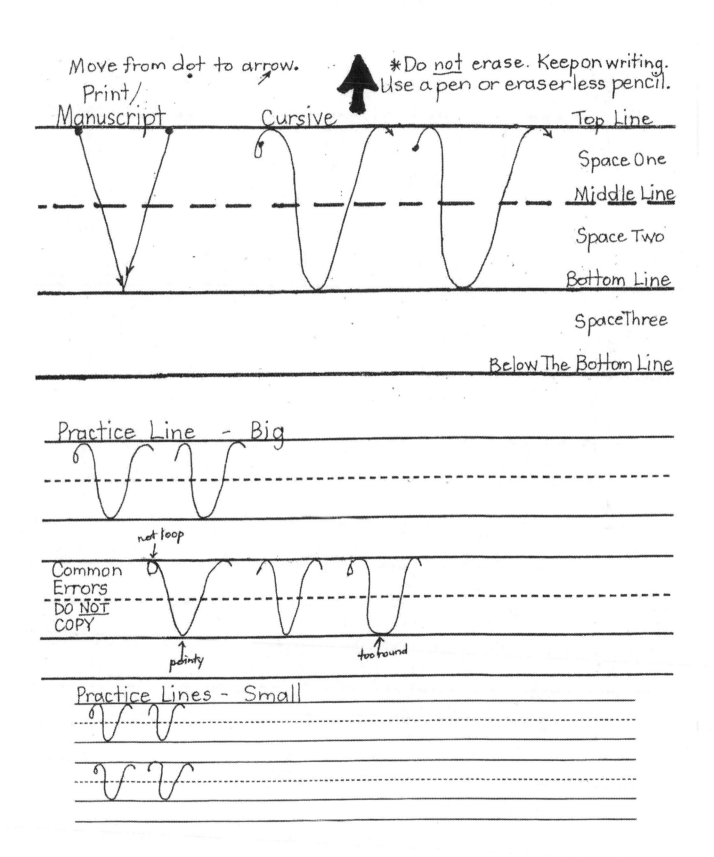

Print/
Manuscript

Cursive

Top Line

Space One

Middle Line

Space Two

Bottom Line

Space Three

Below The Bottom Line

Practice Line - Big

not loop

Common
Errors
DO NOT
COPY

pointy

too round

Practice Lines - Small

Move from dot to arrow.

Print/ Manuscript   Cursive

*Do not erase. Keep on writing.
Use a pen or eraserless pencil.

Top Line

Space One

Middle Line

Space Two

Bottom Line

Space Three

Below The Bottom Line

Practice Line - Big

Common Errors
DO NOT COPY

no retracing   too narrow   too narrow   too long

do not start here

Practice Lines - Small

Move from dot to arrow.

Print/
Manuscript   Cursive   *Do not erase. Keep on writing.
Use a pen or eraserless pencil.

Top Line

Space One

Middle Line

Space Two

Bottom Line

Space Three

Below The Bottom Line

Practice Line - Big

Common
Errors   cross too high
DO NOT
COPY   cross too low

Practice Lines - Small

Move from dot to arrow.

Print/
Manuscript

Cursive

*Do not erase. Keep on writing.
Use a pen or eraserless pencil.

Top Line

Space One

Middle Line

Space Two

Bottom Line

Space Three

Below The Bottom Line

Practice Line - Big

Common
Errors
DO NOT
COPY

too wide

too narrow

too wide
need to cross at
bottom line

Practice Lines - Small

Move from dot to arrow.

*Do not erase. Keep on writing.
Use a pen or eraserless pencil.

Print/
Manuscript

Cursive

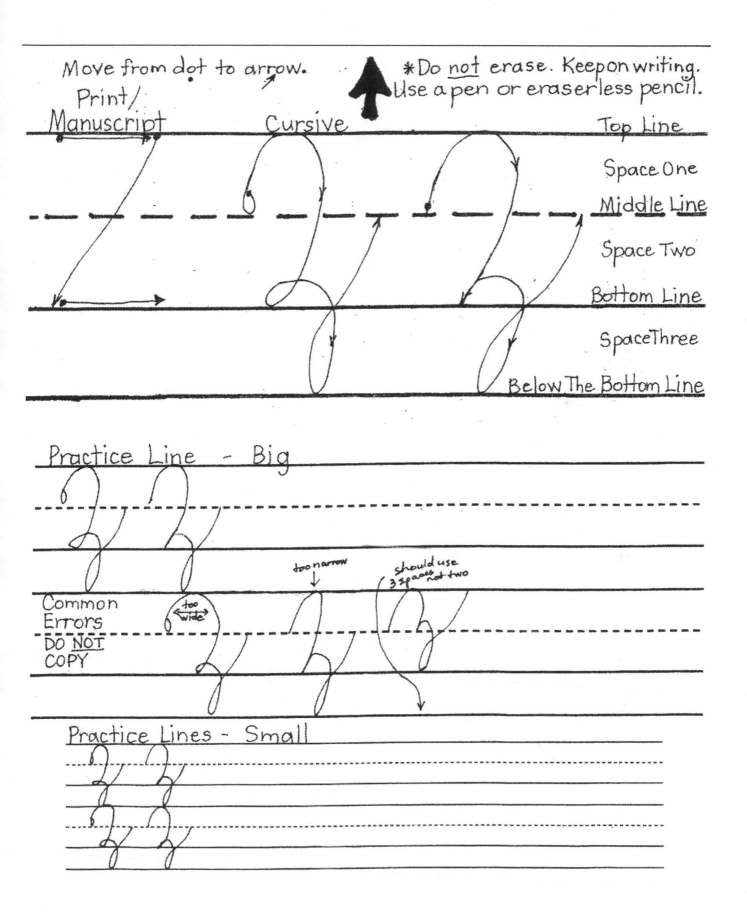

Top Line

Space One

Middle Line

Space Two

Bottom Line

Space Three

Below The Bottom Line

Practice Line - Big

Common
Errors
DO NOT
COPY

too
wide

too narrow

should use
3 spaces not two

Practice Lines - Small

SECTION FOUR

CAPITALS THAT CAN JOIN

Aa Ca Ea Ha Ja

Ka La Ma Na

Qa Ra Ua Ya

Za

CAPITALS THAT DO NOT JOIN

Ba Da Fa Ga La

Oa Pa Sa Ta Va

Wa Xa

Names

Alanna Alden Ashley Ann

Braydon Bernaldo Bella

Cecile Christopher Cher

Darryl Denis Debbie Derek

Elizabeth Edgar Elijah

Fabian Francisco Felix

Names

Gary Gina Gerald Guy

Helen Harrison Harmony

Ikaika Isabella Israel

Josh James Jeff June

Kevin Kaitlin Kenneth

Lindsay Lono Lionel

Names

Michael Marry Marry

Nathan Naomi Natalya

Otto Olivia Oscar Orion

Pamela Patricia Pedro

Queenie Quincy Quentin

Robert René Rodney

Names

Stacy Steven Stephanie

Tommy Terrill Tabitha

Ulysses Usher Victor

Valerie Winslow Walter

Xavier Xander Yolanda

Yvette Zack Zoe Zion

SECTION FIVE

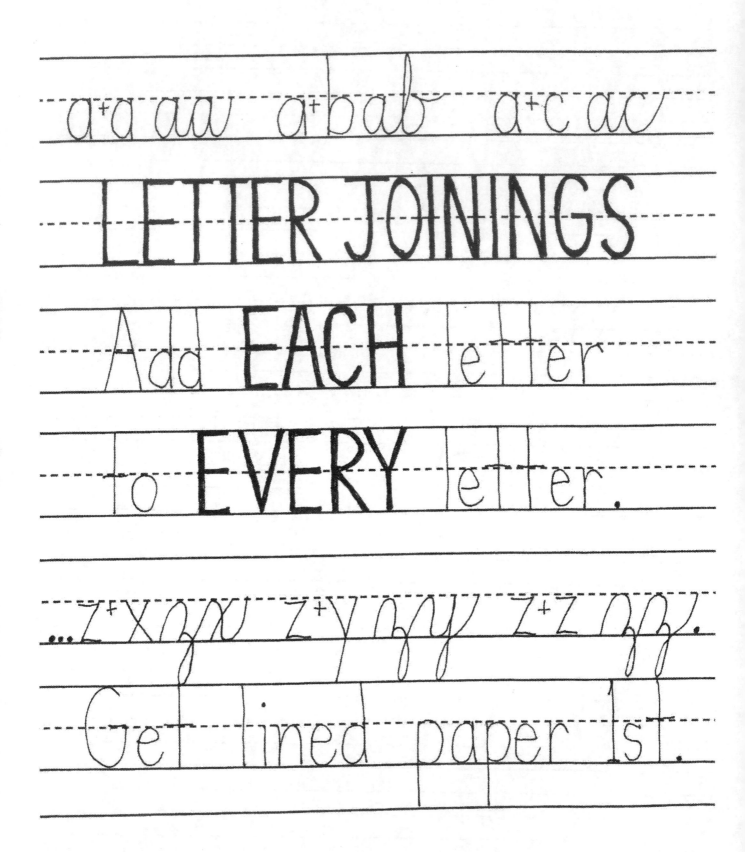

a⁺a aa a⁺b ab a⁺c ac

LETTER JOININGS

Add EACH letter

to EVERY letter.

z⁺x zx z⁺y zy z⁺z zz.

Get lined paper 1st.

aa ab ac ad ae af ag ah

ai aj ak al am an ao ap

aq ar as at au av aw

ax ay az

ba bb bc bd be bf bg

bh bi bj bk bl bm bn

bo bp bq br bs bt bu

bv bw bx by bz

ca cb cc cd ce cf cg

ch ci cj ck cl cm cn

co cp cq cr cs ct cu

cv cw cx cy cz

da db dc dd de df dg

dh di dj dk dl dm dn

do dp dq dr ds dt du

dv dw dx dy dz

ea eb ec ed ee ef eg eh

ei ej ek el em en eo

ep eq er es et eu ev

ew ex ey ez

fa fb fc fd fe ff fg

fh fi fj fk fl fm fn

fo fp fq fr fs ft fu

fv fw fx fy fz

ga gb gc gd ge gf gg

gh gi gj gk gl gm gn

go gp gq gr gs gt gu

gv gw gx gy gz

ha hb hc hd he hf hg

hh hi hj hk hl hm hn

ho hp hq hr hs ht hu

hv hw hx hy hz

ia ib ic id ie if ig ih

ii ij ik il im in io ip

iq ir is it iu iv iw ix

iy iz

ja jb jc jd je jf jg jh

ji jj jk jl jm jn jo

jp jq jr js jt ju jv

jw jx jy jz

ka kb kc kd ke kf kg

kh ki kj kk kl km kn

ko kp kq kr ks kt ku

kv kw kx ky kz

la lb lc ld le lf lg lh

li lj lk ll lm ln lo

lp lq lr ls lt lu lv lw

lx ly lz

ma mb mc md me mf

mg mh mi mj mk ml mm

mn mo mp mq mr ms mt

mu mv mw mx my mz

na nb nc nd ne nf ng

nh ni nj nk nl nm nn

no np nq nr ns nt nu

nv nw nx ny nz

oa ob oc od oe of og oh

oi oj ok ol om on oo op

oq or os ot ou ov ow

ox oy oz

pa pb pc pd pe pf pg

ph pi pj pk pl pm pn

po pp pq pr ps pt pu

pv pw px py pz

qa qb qc qd qe qf qg

qh qi qj qk ql qm qn

qo qp qq qr qs qt qu

qv qw qx qy qz

ra rb rc rd re rf rg

rh ri rj rk rl rm rn

ro rp rq rr rs rt ru

rv rw rx ry rz

sa sb sc sd se sf sg

sh si sj sk sl sm sn

so sp sq sr ss st su

sv sw sx sy sz

ta tb tc td te tf tg

th ti tj tk tl tm tn

to tp tq tr ts tt tu

tv tw tx ty tz

ua ub uc ud ue uf ug

uh ui uj uk ul um un

uo up uq ur us ut uu

uv uw ux uy uz

va vb vc vd ve vf vg

vh vi vj vk vl vm vn

vo vp vq vr vs vt vu

vv vw vx vy vz

wa wb wc wd we wf wg

wh wi wj wk wl wm wn

wo wp wq wr ws wt wuwv

ww wx wy wz

xa xb xc xd xe xf xg

xh xi xj xk xl xm xn

xo xp xq xr xs xt xu

xv xw xx xy xz

ya yb yc yd ye yf yg

yh yi yj yk yl ym yn

yo yp yq yr ys yt yu

yv yw yx yy yz

za zb zc zd ze zf zg

zh zi zj zk zl zm zn

zo zp zq zr zs zt zu

zv zw zx zy zz

Copy 2-sided Laminate

Index

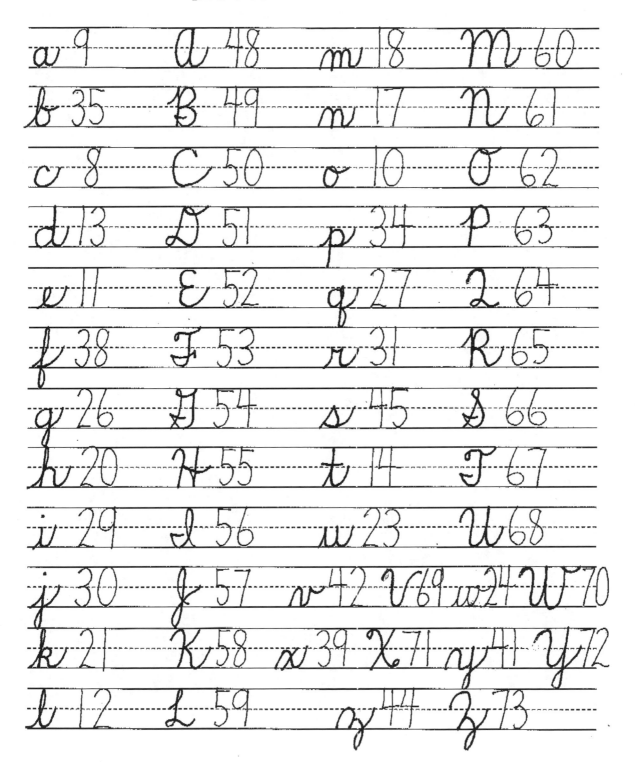

115

DEDICATION

This book is dedicated to my parents, Bernaldo "Happy" Castillio and Elizabeth Patricia Gomes Avillanoza. They have instilled in me honesty, kindness, generosity, and modesty. I love my parents as much as I love my children and grandchildren!

Printed in the United States
by Baker & Taylor Publisher Services